Amelia Island

BOOK OF SECRETS II

Fact vs. Fiction?

Maritime Archaeologist Scott R. Jensen

authorHOUSE®

AuthorHouse™
1663 Liberty Drive
Bloomington, IN 47403
www.authorhouse.com
Phone: 833-262-8899

Published by AuthorHouse 12/13/2021

ISBN: 978-1-6655-3948-7 (sc)
ISBN: 978-1-6655-3966-1 (e)

DEDICATION

It is a pleasure in writing this book to acknowledge Noel Marie Lehman for her continuous encouragement, support and contributions in writing this second publication. Special thanks to my other team members, Matt Batten, Don Gay, William L. Taylor, Candi Nichols, and Gary Czito who all also share the same passion for hunting artifacts. Lastly and so importantly, I also want to acknowledge my parents, whom I love dearly.

CONTENTS

INTRODUCTION

Amelia Island Book of Secrets II

Fact vs. Fiction?

This publication is not written for the academics of the world sitting in their ivory tower; it is written for the average person. This is a sequel to the book, *Amelia Island Book of Secrets.*

There are many secrets on Amelia Island; some are facts, and some are fiction! The author will go chapter by chapter and let the reader decide which are fact and which ones are fiction. (Excluding Chapter 7).

The author shall go into a brief history of Amelia Island; this will help the readers who have not yet read *Amelia Island Book of Secrets* to understand where the island is located and how it is set up geographically.

❧ CHAPTER ONE ❧

History of Amelia Island

THERE IS A PLACE CALLED Amelia Island on the Atlantic Ocean; it known as the *Isle of Eight Flags*… and with good reason. Eight flags have flown over this Island. The French, the Spanish, the British, the Patriots, the Green Cross, the Mexican Republic, the Confederate, and lastly the United States flag.

This is not intended to be a publication on the history of the Island, but merely a review of the history to let the readers know where Amelia Island is located and what secrets it holds. You will be able to understand where you are as the reader, by going through the Island's past.

According to *Environmental Geology Series*, Amelia Island, Florida lies at 30.62' North 81.46' West. The Island is 4 miles in width and 13.3 miles in length.

Amelia Island was formed from river deposited alluvium that was piled up by wind, ocean, and storms.

According to *Yesterday's Reflections,* the French Huguenot leader, Jean Ribault, who landed on the island in 1562, recorded the first contact with Europeans in the Amelia Island area. Ribault named it *Isle de Mai* (Island of May) (Johannes 2000).

Although the Spanish had originally claimed La Florida for their empire, this did not prevent the French from trying and succeeding to break the Spanish hold on this part of the New World. Spain had claimed the area in 1513, however, that did not prevent the French colonist from landing.

Colonists were not only seeking land for France, but also refuge from religious and political persecution. Though Ribault and his company didn't remain, the Huguenots returned again in 1564 under Rene de Laudonniere, who was a commander on another return voyage (Amelia Island Museum of History 2009).

According to *The European Discovery of America*, the second colony constructed was Fort Caroline in North Eastern Florida in 1562. Spanish troops led by Pedro Menendez de Aviles slaughtered the French settlers in order to regain the territory the Spanish had claimed in previous years (Morison 1974).

According to *The Indians of Amelia Island*, the first Spanish reign lasted from 1565 to 1763. The local Timucuan natives' numbers started to decline due to the influx of European disease and the disruption of their lifestyle. Though the Timucuan numbers were once 30,000 they were completely extinct within approximately 100 years of first contact with the Europeans (Jaccard 2000).

According to *Florida Archaeology*, the British settlements in the north took an interest in the area because of the naturally deep ports and the strategic trade route location. Georgia's Governor, James Oglethorpe named the Island "Amelia" in 1735 in honor Princess Amelia, daughter of King George II.

Though the British named the Island "Amelia", it did not fall into British hands until Spanish Florida was traded for British Cuba in 1763. During the time of British rule, which lasted until 1783, the Island was named Egmont. In 1783, the Second Treaty of Paris ended the French Revolutionary War and returned Florida to Spain. British inhabitants of Florida had to leave the province within 18 months unless they swore allegiance to Spain. In 1811, surveyor George J. F. Clarke platted the town "Fernandina" who had chosen the name in honor of King Ferdinand VII of Spain.

To drive out the Spanish, the Patriots of Amelia Island, an independent group of American civilians backed by the United States government, seized control of the island and raised their flag on March 17, 1812.

The very next day, the Patriots ceded Amelia Island to the United States. However, Spain's strong protest forced the U.S. to relinquish its new possession, in light of the impending War of 1812 with England.

In 1817, a Scotsman named Sir Gregor MacGregor, with the support of some key Americans, ran the Spanish off the island and raised the Green Cross of Florida flag. However, because of lack of reinforcements and funds, MacGregor left the island and his lieutenants took charge.

These lieutenants made a deal with French Luis Aury, a soldier in the Mexican Revolution, in order to gain support to maintain control. However, Aury, in return for giving them support, wanted to command the Island and therefore raised the Mexican Republic flag.

According to *Florida Archaeology* the town came into such a state of bedlam that the U.S. government sent gunboats, took control, and held Amelia Island in trust for Spain until Florida became a U.S. territory on July 10, 1821 (Fairbanks and Mcanich 1980).

According to *Fort Clinch*, the Confederates took control of Fort Clinch, which had been started by the Federals and later abandoned because of the outbreak of the Civil War.

The Confederate flag was raised at Fort Clinch in April 1861. In less than a year, Union forces surrounded the Fort, and Union control held throughout the remainder of the War (Gooding 1974). In the time period from 1870 to 1910, many wealthy Americans made their home on Amelia Island. In New Fernandina they constructed many elegant Victorian style homes.

This boom was due to the shipping industry and the fact many New Yorkers were coming down by steamboat to enjoy the climate. In 1890, Standard Oil co-founder Henry Flagler opened up the railroad in Florida. Flagler detoured much of the tourist traffic to St. Augustine and places farther south on Amelia Island in the 1900s.

Subsequently, two paper mills were located on the island, which provided an additional boost to the economy. These mills remain functioning today! In the 1970's Amelia Island Plantation and the Ritz-Carlton were built as resorts with a natural setting. This resulted in the Island being recognized as a tourist area and it continues to be to this day.

❊ CHAPTER TWO ❊

More Treasure Stories

Old Town

I N OLD FERNANDINA / OLD TOWN there are many treasure stories that have come to the authors attention. Old Town (as we will continue to refer to the area as) and the surrounding areas have been known to be a haven for treasure.

This first story involves Old Town and a house that was being built in the 1980's on the North End of Amelia Island. A construction crew who were prepping the site, started to excavate and found something out of the ordinary. They then took a long lunch and never came back…

The story goes that they found a massive treasure chest while digging the site! They split the treasure up and went on their way.

Fact vs Fiction?

Old Town & Surrounding Areas

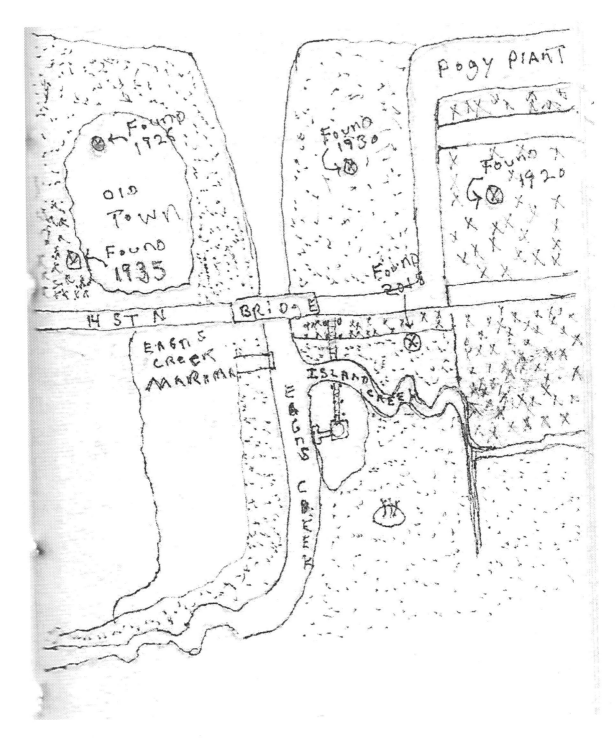

Figure 1

The Shipwreck *Alvarez*

The *Alvarez* was a wreck located on the North End of Amelia Island. During the Civil War it was a supply ship with a gold payroll. This ship was a prime target for divers and treasure hunters.

There was one diver who consistently dove this wreck. When he was off of work, he was diving! He eventually discovered a safe he hoped the gold was in. After breaking the safe open he saw wonderful things…. gold!

He took a five-gallon bucket and transferred the gold into the container. Later, he took it to a dive shop to show it off. Eventually, he quit his job and never was see again.

Fact vs Fiction?

Amelia Island Plantation

The "Plantation" is an oceanfront community on the South End of Amelia Island. When construction of the houses started, workers and builders were everywhere. What do they do first when building a house? They excavate! Many people are adamant that excavations were conducted on the golf course near the ocean. I will let the reader decide!

During said excavations, two separate chests were located. The author presumes these chests contained gold. They were found during deep excavations (over eight feet in depth). What does the reader think?

As stated, the "Plantation" is on the South End of the Amelia Island, it was founded in 1971. It is now owned by Omni Hotel & Resorts.

Fact vs Fiction?

Beach Patrol

Many years ago, the author worked as an educator at a local school. It was awesome! When the school year was over in the summer, I would hunt for long forgotten shipwrecks.

While I was diving as a Maritime Archaeologist, I would go on the Research Vessel *"Polly-L"* with a dollar in my pocket, and after 12 weeks, leave with that same dollar in my pocket. Everything was provided for me! It was a great vessel and we were all having a blast! Then something happened… I got a strange phone message. (I leave my phone in my cabin while diving).

It was from an individual the author had known for many years. He was on the shore admiring the vessel, when the Beach Patrol stopped him. He stated that the Beach Patrol asked a strange question… "Is Archaeologist Scott Jensen on the boat?" (At the time the vessel was out of shore approximately 1 mile).

I was on the vessel at the time. The Beach Patrol Officer said she had found two gold coins on the Southern Shores of Amelia Island. The Officer then proceeds to tell my friend she was a Resource Officer at the author's school (These were Police Officers assigned to each school in Nassau County, Florida).

The Officer said that I would know her, as she had short blonde hair and worked at my school. (They would change Officer's every couple of years). Trouble was, after 20 years of being an educator, too many were blondes with short hair!

Ultimately, I got my friends phone message, however, I never got to see those gold coins!

What does the reader think?

Fact vs Fiction?

<u>Spring</u>

Bernard Romans published a book titled *A Concise Natural History of East and West Florida*, it is not necessarily an "easy" read, but it is fact filled! It was published in 1775, and it starts from Amelia Island and goes around to the West Coast of Florida.

Romans' map led to the identity of the 1715 Plate Fleet (Plate means treasure); Sebastian-Vero Beach area which is now known as the "Treasure Coast". He was a cartographer, surveyor, a botanist, a naturalist, scientist, and explorer.

What does have it have to do with Amelia Island's Secrets? Romans states: "On Amelia Island near the sea, is a very good spring, which makes fine stream for some miles, dividing the island almost in two." This is Egan's Creek.

The Spanish used that spring to gather water. A gentleman in modern times found an olive jar full of coins by that spring. I was talking to this gentleman about his find at *The Maritime Museum of Amelia Island*, when he noticed my picture on the wall as THE Archeologist, and he just walked out of the museum!

Fact vs Fiction?

Jeweler's Furnace

In a museum far away, tucked in a corner, lies a mystery. *The Maritime Museum of Amelia Island* in Fernandina Beach, Florida, has what is called a "Jeweler's Furnace".

The Furnace was used to test the purity of precious metals. The box was filled with coal which an would create an internal combustion that would melt down the precious metals. The Jeweler could then assess if it the metals were real or fake.

The Furnace was found on the South End of the Island by a metal detectorist and diver in 1992. He was hired by *Old World Treasure Quest* (currently *Amelia Research and Recovery*) and what a great find it was! The Furnace would have been on a ship of immense wealth and was from a Colonial period shipwreck (approximately 1607 to 1776).

Fact vs Fiction?

Jeweler's Furnace

Figure 2

Jeweler's Furnace II

Figure 3

Illustration of the Jeweler's Furnace

Figure 4

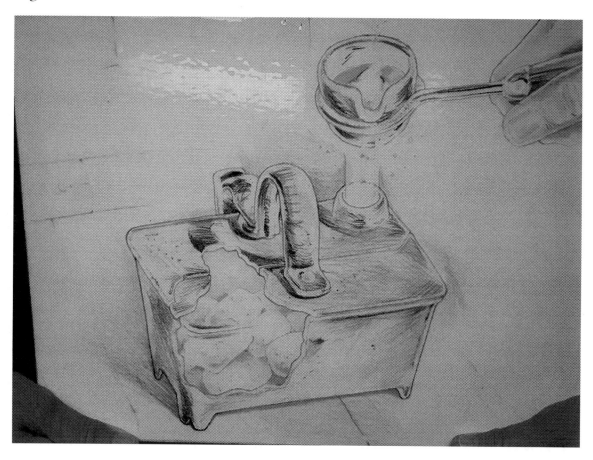

The Palace Saloon

On Amelia Island is the oldest, continuously running bar in the State of Florida. It is called the Palace Saloon and it was opened in 1903. The saloon has a massive carved mahogany bar which was built in a Victorian style.

The Saloon burned in 1999, but not completely; yet enough to warrant a rebuild. Strangely enough, the fire did not burn the beautiful mahogany bar. The Saloon was built better than ever.

It has been said, while the Firefighters were on the job pulling the walls down, they pulled out treasure. This treasure included a dagger, gold, and silver coins in a leather sack!

Fact vs Fiction?

The Palace Saloon

Figure 4.2

The Pirate on guard at the Palace Saloon

Figure 44

Interior of the Palace Saloon

Figure 4.6

CHAPTER THREE

Treasure Puzzles

The Story of Captain William Kidd

CAPTAIN KIDD WAS IN THE author's previous publication titled *Amelia Island Book of Secrets*; however, I will not go as far in depth of the history of Kidd within this publication.

Captain William Kidd, or as he was called by the people who knew him; Captain Kidd. Kidd was a Privateer on Amelia Island. A Privateer was sanctioned by a particular country to attack other countries' ships. (A Privateer is similar to a Buccaneer). Captain Kidd was said to have a fortune in gold and silver hidden in several locations on Amelia Island.

Kidd was executed for piracy in May, 1701 in London, England. Before he was hanged, he supposedly gave his wife a cryptic message on a piece of parchment. The message was a series of numbers as follows:

44106818

If a person can decipher this message, you could be a very rich person indeed!

.... But only if you come to search on Amelia Island!

Fact vs Fiction?

Written in Stone

Our treasure hunting group was heading into the "jungles" of Amelia when we found a huge tree. Nothing special about the tree, you say…or is there? We then noticed something on the ground. Rocks, nothing special about rocks you say… Until one of our group noticed a stone on the ground with an inscription carved on it!

Our consensus was that it was a map! This map described the location of treasure. The map was in great detail… It contained rivers, creeks, and jungles. If you look at it very closely it has an X.

X marks the spot…… The author will let the reader decide!

Fact vs Fiction?

Member of our team exploring the "Jungles" of Amelia

Figure 5

Trees & Rocks

Figure 6

Trees & Rocks II

Figure 7

Map in Stone

Figure 8

Map in Stone II

Figure 9

Son of Padra John Puzzle

16 Figure 3 left

Can't go forward

Can't go back

Redman rock burns

Take the pieces to the place

of Padra John

There receive 100 gold bullion

Fact vs Fiction?

Aury's Treasure Map

Luis Aury was a pirate and he had eight prizes in the Amelia Island harbor. Prizes were ships seized by pirates. Aury supposedly had several treasure chests hid around Amelia Island.

The author knows that much of the real wealth came from seizing slave ships and selling them in Georgia. I, however, cannot (or, perhaps will not) verify whether chests of gold, silver, and jewelry were ever on the island! However, stranger things have been on found this island!

According to "Ballads of the Buccaneer Trail" the following page contains Aury's Treasure map! (Figure 10)

What does the reader think?

Fact vs Fiction?

Aury's Treasure Map

Figure 10

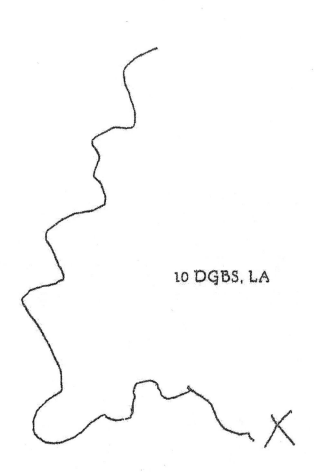

10 DGBS, LA

SSW FR FSC, 2 LG, SHBK, L 100 P   15 DGBN,

LOKTR, MK2CH,2 ARP ASAZ, 2LB TPO 6DJL.

CHAPTER FOUR

Mound of Amelia

O<small>N</small> E<small>GAN'S</small> C<small>REEK</small> G<small>REENWAY</small> (<small>NEAR</small> the Creek) there is a giant mound. Its measure's roughly 30 feet in diameter and about 14 feet in height. As stated in *Amelia Island Book of Secrets* there once were middens and mounds all over the Island.

Middens are piles often containing shells and trash; mounds are for burials. (In this area Timucuan Indians are presumed buried in the mounds). In the following photographs the reader will see how massive this mound is.

Mound

Figure 11

Mound Photograph II

Figure 12

Author on the Mound

Figure 13

Author on Mound II

Figure 14

The Author first had to get to the mound. Our group brought a ramp to get across the creek. When our group finally got access to the creek, it was rough terrain and environment.

As the reader can see, this mound is huge! I roughly checked the dimensions again and started to climb. It was an amazing view on the top of the mound. You could see the entire landscape, birds, and all sorts of animals.

As an Archeologist, I made a cardinal mistake... I went to the site a second time by myself. You always work in pairs; but on this day I did not. I paid the price for going in alone. It looked like normal land. It had small trees, flowers, and grass. It was not...it was quicksand, and it pulled me down to my chest; I was alone.

I struggled to get out. It took two hours to get out of the swamp mud, when I finally got out on solid land, I had no energy left. No energy means just lying down struggling to even stand up. It took another hour to get my body upright.

I was scratched and cut all over my body; bleeding. Ultimately, I took a deer trail out without any problems. I finally got to my vehicle, I was full of swamp mud, from my head to my toes. I learned a big lesson; always take a member of your team!

So much for my mistakes, in my opinion, it is a modern mound. There were huge stones around the mound and in the nearby Creek. Modern trash all around. It has been said it was previously a dump site.

That brings up the question, why was it the only mound on the dump site? To the author's experience and expertise, without digging it up, it is a modern mound; however, what does the reader think?

(Just don't go alone!)

Fact vs Fiction?

CHAPTER FIVE

Tunnel

T HIS IS A STORY OF two different buildings... but are they truly separate? They are the Fernandina Beach Courthouse and the local Post Office. The following photograph is of the Court House. The Court House was built in 1891 and is taller than the Post Office.

When I was young man in 2002, I watched them working on the bell tower of the Courthouse, when they discovered a book. I do not know what it was titled or where it went, but its' discovery is what led me to be passionate about archaeology!

As the legend goes, there is a tunnel connecting the two buildings. The reader has the task of determining one thing... Is there a **Tunnel** running underground connecting the Courthouse to the local United States Post Office?

Court House

Figure 15

This is the United States Post Office in Fernandina Beach and it is an amazing building. It was it built in 1911, and it is recognized in the National Register of Historic Places. It has four stories and a loft (even though the historical placards say only three). So, let's take a look at the following photographs.

Fernandina Beach Post Office on Centre Street

Figure 16

Fernandina Beach Post Office

Figure 17

The Post Office (first story) remains as it was in its' early years. Old wood, gorgeous patina, and it looks as if you are in a Museum.

Interior of Post Office

Figure 18

The second floor, above the actual Post Office's first story, makes you feel like you are in a different time in history. It has an old Courtroom on this floor, the paint is peeling and there are sections that do not have power. It also had law offices and offices of many other types.

Court Room

Figure 19

Second Story of the Court House

Figure 20

Stay with the author, as we are continuing to "go up the stairs" to the third story. It contains a walk-in Safe. There are Safes everywhere in the building. It was also a Customs House in use until approximately the 1940's. It also has a loft; this is a huge, beautiful, historical building!

Safe

Figure 21

Interior of the Safe

Figure 22

Looking out of the third story window

Figure 23

Not everyone knows that the building has a basement in it. This creates a topic of controversy. Is there a **tunnel** that goes under Centre Street to the even older Fernanda Beach Court House? Some people say yes! Some people say no!

It has power for lights as you go down to the stairs. However, there are no lights towards the front of the basement. The basement is dark and dingy and faces toward Centre Street. It is awesome! The author will show you the controversial "tunnel" leading towards Centre Street.

Time to look at a series of photographs to help the reader understand what is contained within this controversial basement of the Post Office.

Post Office Basement Photograph

Figure 24

Post Office Basement Photograph II

Figure 25

Post Office Basement Photograph III

Figure 26

What do you see? I see a tunnel!... I could not possibly know what it was used for, but the story goes that it was used to transfer items (or people?) from the Courthouse to the to the interior of the Customs Office.

Supposedly, they transported precious metals, jewelry, packages, or perhaps it used to protect or transport humans in secret? The tunnel was filled with concrete when Centre Street was bricked. I can't confirm any information other than the stories and legends stated above.

What does the reader think?

Fact vs Fiction?

❉ CHAPTER SIX ❉

Maps of Amelia Island

MAPS HAVE BEEN USED THROUGHOUT history to guide people to places, land, sea, or perhaps to find long lost treasure. Maps were made out of anything that they could find to transcribe on.

Animal skin (parchment), papyrus, rocks, and basically anything that could be written on. The earliest maps date to the 5th Centuries BC. Modern maps are on printed paper or Global Positioning System (GPS).

The GPS uses a series of satellites to place you on the exact spot you are seeking! The author will show a series of maps. Look at them carefully and try to locate Amelia Island, shipwrecks, or can the reader locate possible treasure locations?

Old Maps of Amelia Island I

Figure 27

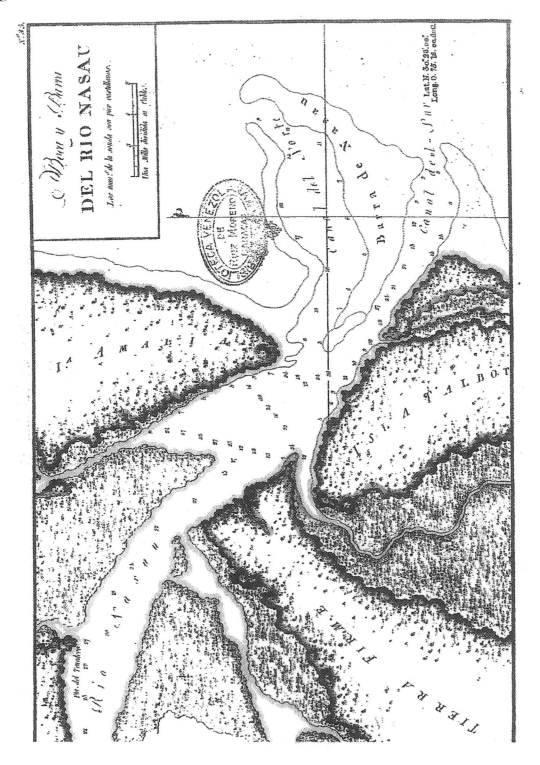

Old Maps from Amelia Island II

Figure 28

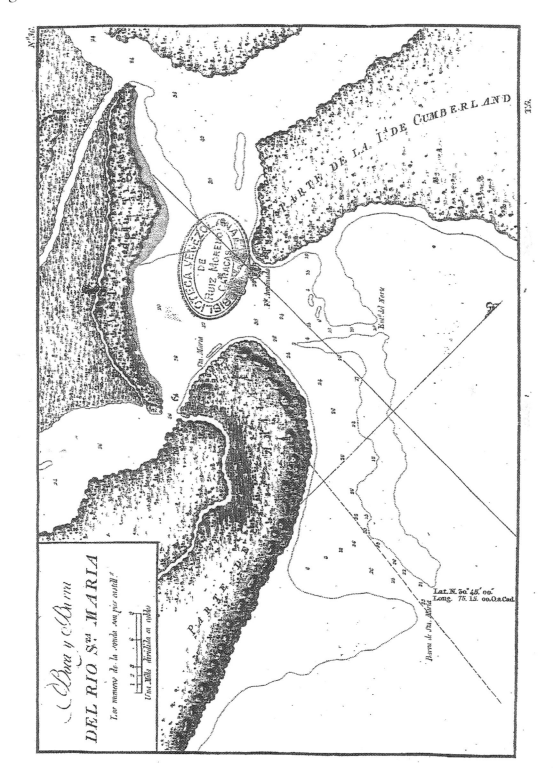

Old Maps of Amelia Island III

Figure 29

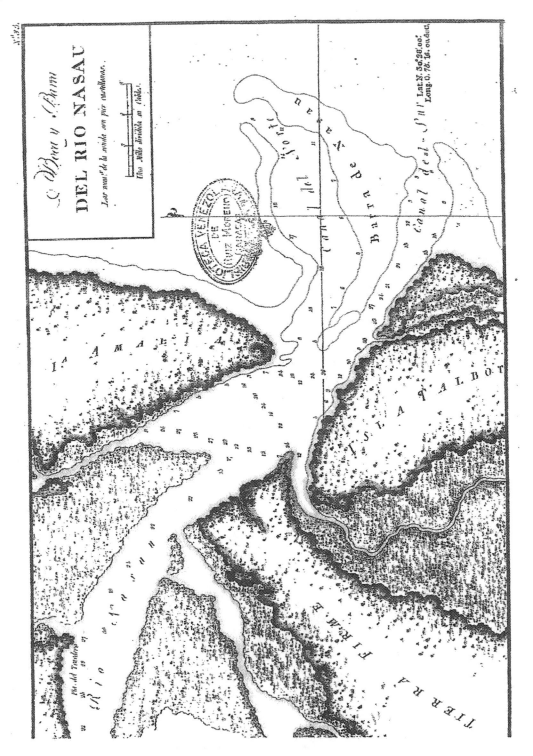

Old Maps from Amelia Island IV

Figure 30

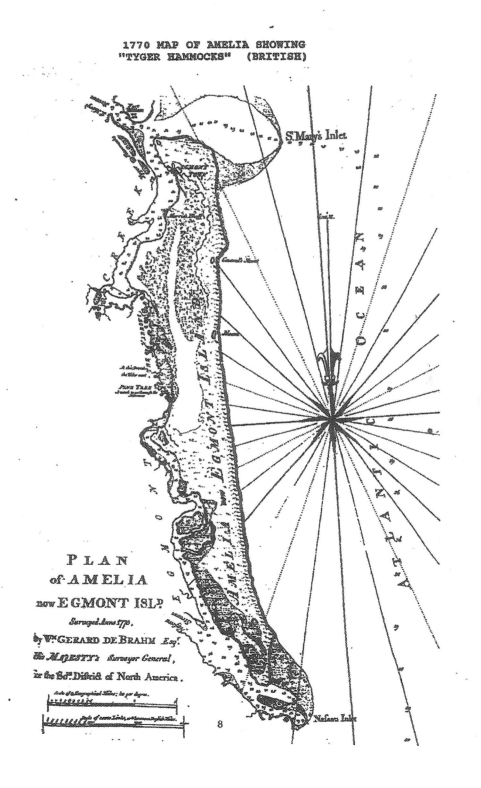

Old Map of Amelia Island V

Figure 31

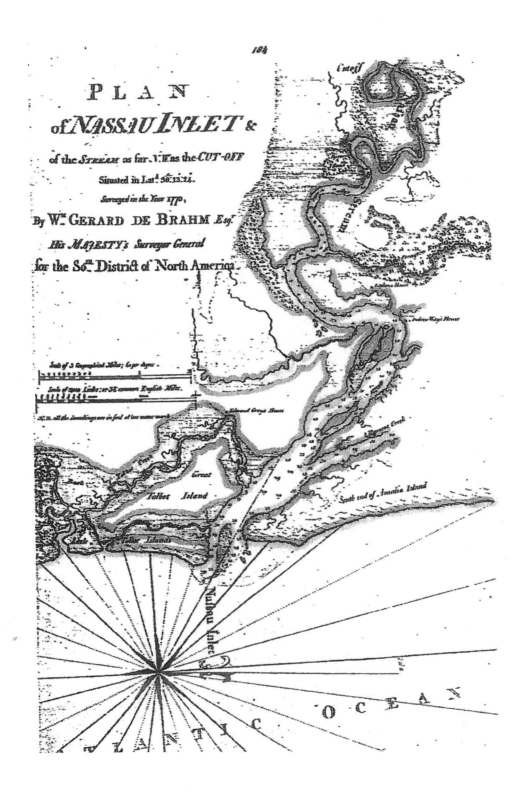

Old Maps from Amelia Island VI

Figure 32

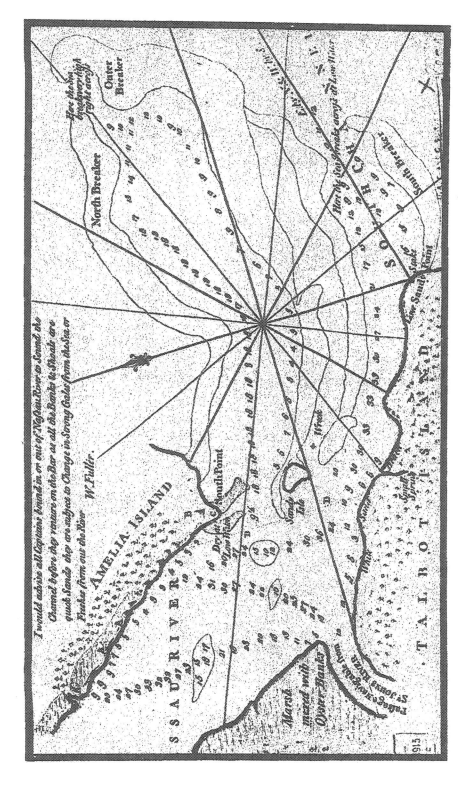

Old Maps from Amelia Island VII

Figure 33

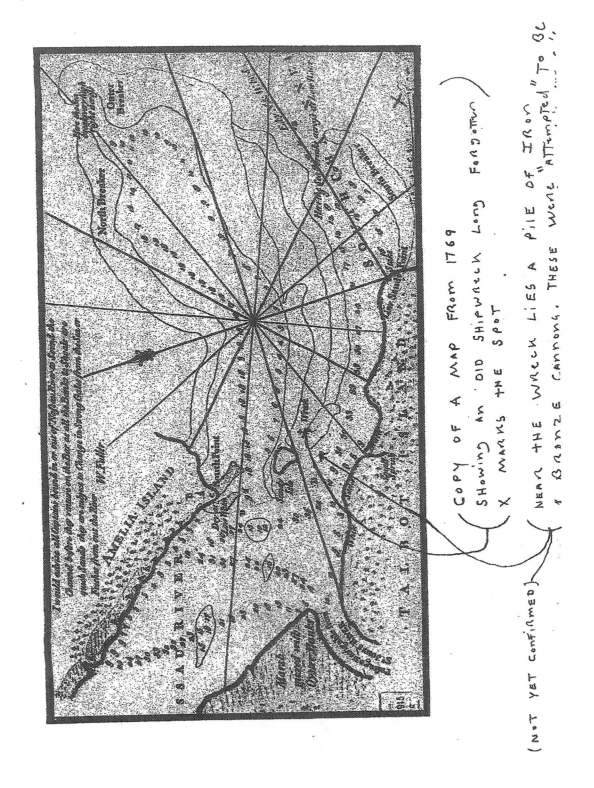

The previous examples are of old maps of land, sea, and the surrounding areas of Amelia Island. On the sea, the difference between life and death is contained in these maps. If they were not accurate in the Nassau Sound, a captain could risk his ship, his life, and his crew!

Many shipwreck's have sunk in the Nassau Sound. Sand bars shifting every day, low tides and zero visibility. Tides are so low it is very dangerous to try to maneuver ships through them. Even the professionals have a hard time getting through the Nassau Sound.

For example, according to *A Concise Natural History of East and West Florida,* Bernard Romans states "A plan of these two inlets exactly from my original survey of this island, (Amelia Island) was some time ago published by Capt. *Fuller,* who sounded the bars, but he has placed the soundings rather too deep, both within and without" (This was published in 1775).

In Figure 32 & 33 are *Captain Fullers* maps. He may have caused several shipwrecks on the Nassau Sound with his erroneous sounding (sounding is the depth of the water). In Figure 34 is a current map drawn by John Poppin (Field Archeologist) of the Nassau Sound with shipwreck's contained within.

Current Map of the Nassau Sound VIII

Figure 34

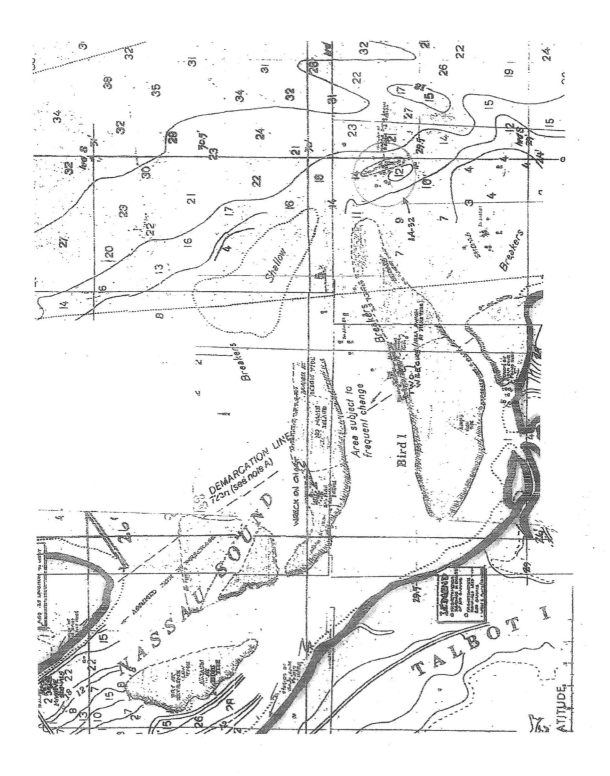

The good thing about a map... it can get you out of danger and into a place of safety if is drawn correctly!

The maps shown are very old in nature, some go back to the 1600's. Did the reader find Amelia Island on the maps? Did the reader find shipwrecks on some of the maps? (The author will give the reader a hint; three maps of the Nassau Sound have at least one shipwreck).

Fact vs Fiction?

CHAPTER SEVEN

Government Destruction

THIS IS NOT A FACT VS. Fiction chapter; this is about government destruction. The government has destroyed many shipwrecks at all levels. Local, State, and Federal shipwrecks & artifacts have been destroyed.

Artifacts

Eugene Lyon Ph.D. was a Historian and the foremost expert of Spanish history in the world. He lived in St Augustine, Florida and was the head of the of the Department of History at Flagler Collage.

In Figure 35 &36 you see Dr. Lyon on Amelia Island.

Dr. Lyon examining Artifacts of Amelia Island

Figure 35

Dr. Lyon determined it to date in the Colonial Period due to the wooden trunnels, and iron fittings.

Artifacts left to Rot

Figure 36

Most all of the ribs that are
in the state park are currently
being destroyed by termites &
ants. The state park will not
release them to be preserved.

That was the first time the author witnessed government destruction. The
first time the author had witnessed the refusal of a State Park to accept an offer
to conserve parts of shipwrecks. This, however was not the first time it has
happened.

Keel

The author received a call from the head of Fernandina Beach Police Department. He said something had washed up on shore and the Officer was aware that I was a local Archaeologist.

I ironically had been tracking this artifact for months. It was from Fort Clinch (a Fort located on the Northern shores of Amelia Island) and it was a piece of a keel from a shipwreck.

It migrated down the shore toward my beach house. I went to the beach and wrote a report on the artifacts and took some photographs.

Look at Figures 37-40

Keel Section

Figure 37

Keel Section II

Figure 38

Keel Section III

Figure 39

Keel Section IV

Figure 40

Rough Archaeological Drawing of the Keel Section

Figure 40.1

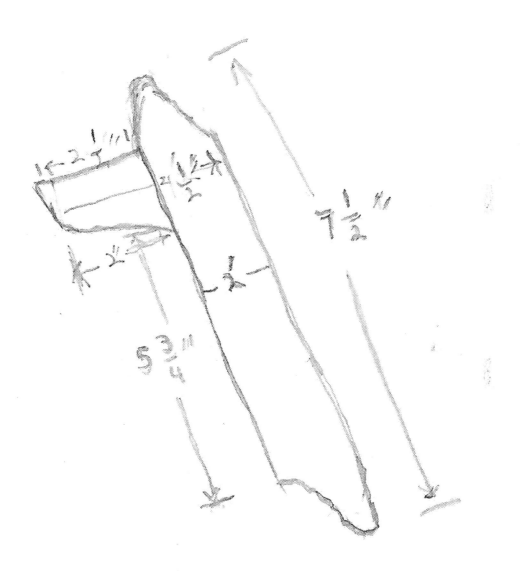

I called the Police Chief and explained what it was. The keel migrated up to the Main Beach. It made the newspapers and the internet. Then, it just suddenly disappeared!

I learned that a dump truck was seen on the Main Beach loading it up and taking it to the dump. Wow! Now that is an awful example of local government destruction.

Shipwreck at Ponte Vedra Beach

In 2018, a shipwreck was uncovered up on the shores of Ponte Vedra Beach. Out of St Augustine came a group from the lighthouse. It is called Lighthouse Archaeological Maritime Program (LAMP).

They determined it was an 1850's shipwreck because of the saw cuts on the lumber. LAMP did an awesome 3-dimensional (3D) scan of the ship. Like others artifacts before, it just disappeared!

The Shipwreck located on Ponta Vedera Beach

Figure 41

XX

Figure 42

This Shipwreck was moved to Guana Preserve area then deposited on the ground. It was close to water, but was never put in the water! Anything that is in saltwater environment, whether buried under the beach or in the ocean, is protected from the destructive power of the oxygen in the atmosphere.

Once that protective layer is removed that is when the deterioration starts. Look at Figure 43, it is a shame that the State does not protect these artifacts!

Rotting Shipwreck Hull

Figure 43

Rocks

The author dove a shipwreck site and it was awesome! When the Research Vessel *Polly-L* excavation blew the sand off, we discovered it was mostly intact. As I put on his dive gear, I knew it would be something special.

I went to the boat and dove into the interior of the vessel. I was touching history. This was the only intact shipwreck the author had ever been in. Half the deck was gone, it had erosion tubes (people used them to control beach erosion) around it and it was only about 70 feet off the shore (depending on the tide).

See the Vessel in Figure 44

Archaeologist Drawing of suspected 1800's Shipwreck (Barge?)

Archaeologist Drawing of suspected 1800's Shipwreck (Barge?)

Figure 44

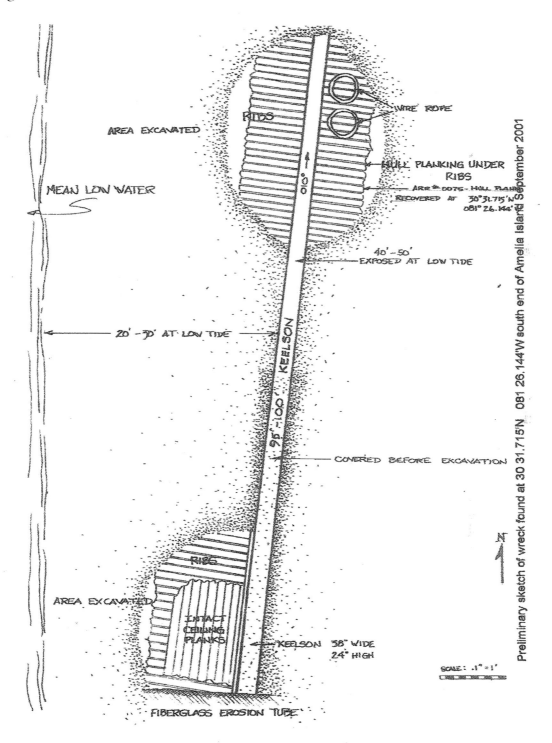

Rocks

Figure 45

Rock II

Figure 46

I suspect the U.S. Army Corps of Engineers (USACE) put the rocks on the shipwreck. You can't do anything without the USACE permission. The author surmises the rocks were put there during a beach renourishment project.

So, it too disappeared!

Government destruction is everywhere. Not just in Florida, the author suspects it is all over the Nation. The Local government does not know what the State Government is doing, and the Federal Government does not know what the what the State is doing and so on...

CHAPTER EIGHT

Archaeology in Motion

THE AUTHOR OWNS AND RUNS the company *Archaeology in Motion*. I have had a great time over the years! However, no archaeologist knows everything. I have had disagreements with many of my professional colleagues. I always try to be professional; that being said however, the more educated you are, the more you think you are right! The author has had many disagreements with different people.

Biologists who think they are an archaeologist, investors who think they are an archaeologist. I have felt sorry for these people, it takes a minimum of six years of college to become an Archaeologist in the State of Florida, and that is **IF** you can convince the State to "play nice" in their sand box!

So, the author has decided to let you, the reader, be the Archaeologist!

Fact vs. Fiction?

These are some of the stories of Amelia Island, Florida. The underlined Fact vs. Fiction are the author opinions. "Not enough Info" states I have no idea if this is true. If it states "Fact" & "Not enough Info" it is based on actual information but the author has no idea if it true.

As the reader of this publication you can decide. Amelia Island has many stories, and still holds many secrets!

Chapter Four: Mound of Amelia

Mound of Amelia   Fact vs. Fiction (Not enough Info)

Chapter Five: Tunnel

Tunnel   Fact vs. Fiction (Not enough Info)

Chapter Six: Maps of Amelia Island

Maps of Amelia Island   Fact vs. Fiction

Chapter Seven: Government Destruction

Government Destruction   Not eligible!

Chapter Eight: The reader is in Chapter Eight!

EPILOGUE

This is not Fact vs. Fiction; these photographs are ones that the author found interesting! A member of the team found something rather strange.

He got a metal detector hit on a tree. Tracing it down the tree, the team member identified it as the root coming out of the tree. Thinking he had found an artifact from years past, he dug under the root and on top of the root to no avail.

It was inside the root!

Tree Root

Epilogue 1

Beer can inside the Root

Epilogue 2

The following photographs are of a member of our team on his quest to find a treasure chest on Amelia Island. The member of our team was sure he found it!

Treasure Chest

Epilogue 3

Not so Fast

Epilogue 4

Our team member thought he had found a treasure chest! He put survey flags on each corner of the chest and started to dig. Ouch! There was no chest; however, that being said, there were two nice bent pins he had found in the shape of a treasure chest!

Epilogue 5

It was a day like any other on the Southern shores of Amelia Island and during the night something strange happen. A hole appeared at daybreak. It was huge! Some people thought they had found a treasure chest, others stated that hole was just beautiful! It took a bulldozer to fill the hole as it was eight foot deep. Hmmm...........

What does the reader think?

REFERENCES CITED

Amelia Island Museum of History. <u>The Historic Splendor of Amelia Island,</u> Fernandina Beach, Florida. Amelia Island Museum of History. 1997.

Archeology in Motion, Inc. 2021.

Fairbanks, Charles H, and Jerald T Mcanich.
<u>Florida Archaeology</u>, Academic Press. Orlando, Florida. 1918.

Gooding, William. <u>Fort Clinch</u> Manuscript distributed by The Florida Department of Natural Resources, State Parks Division. Fernandina Beach Florida. 1974.

Lyon, Eugene, Personal Communication. 2018.

<u>Jewelers Furnace</u>, The Maritime Museum of Amelia Island. 1992.

Jaccard, Lawrence D. <u>Indians of Amelia Island</u>, Lexington Ventures Inc. Fernandina Beach, Florida. 2000.

Johannes, Jan. <u>Yesterday's Reflections</u>, Lexington Ventures Inc. Fernandina Beach, Florida. 2000.

Jensen, Scott. <u>Amelia Island Book of Secrets</u>. AuthorHouse. 2021.

<u>Maps</u>. The Maritime Museum of Amelia Archives, Fernandina Beach, Florida. 2000.

Morison, Samuel. <u>The European Discovery of America.</u> Oxford University Press. New York. 1974.

Scott, Thomas M. <u>Environmental Geology Series</u>: Jacksonville Sheet. Florida Bureau of Geology Map Series No. 89. Tallahassee, Florida

Smith, Denney. <u>Ballads of the Buccaneer Trail</u>. The Hamilton Press. Fernandina Beach, Florida. 1990.

<u>Polly-L</u>. Amelia Research & Recovery, Inc. 2001.

Poppin, John. Amelia Research & Recovery, LLC. 2014.

Old World Treasure Quest, Inc. 1992.

Romans, Bernard. <u>A CONCISE Natural History of East and West Florida</u>. Published in 1775.

Woodard, Colin. The Republic of Pirates, Harcourt, Inc. 2007.

PHOTOS & ILLUSTRATIONS

APPRECIATION PAGE

Thanks to Noel Marie Lehman & Pixi-Pocket for continuing to be my Muses during the creation and writing of this publication.

Thanks to *The Maritime Museum of Amelia Island.*

Thanks to Field Archaeologist John Poppin for the use of his map.

INDEX